Easy Grammar for Kids
Most Easy Way to Learn

Bandana Ojha

Introduction

This English grammar book for kids provides guidelines for choosing words, arrangement of words, and punctuation of sentences. Lesson by lesson, this book provides basic instruction in the ten parts of speech—nouns, pronouns, verbs, adverbs, adjectives, articles, prepositions, conjunctions, contractions and interjections. We do most of our thinking with word symbols. If we cannot arrange word symbols correctly, we probably cannot think clearly and probably cannot communicate effectively.

This grammar book is the perfect resource for every kid who wants to produce clear, concise, and grammatically excellent writing. It will help kids to understand the basic English grammar and develop interest for advance learning. They can become more effective writer and good communicator in their school.

Table of Contents

Chapter-1

NOUN

Definition-

Noun is a word that is name of something, such as a person, animal, place, thing, quality, idea, or action

Types of nouns: -

Common noun

Proper noun

Concrete noun

Abstract noun

Countable noun

Uncountable noun

Collective noun

Singular noun

Plural noun

Common noun:

Common noun is generic noun. It names people, place, animal, things or idea that is not specific.

Examples: -

Doctor

Teacher

More Examples: -

Mechanics, Artist, Baby, Mechanics, Dentist, Lawyer, Man, Woman, Boy, Girl, Door, Watch, Train, Truck, Mountain, Airport, Market, Hotel, Hospital, Church, School, Whale, Tiger, etc.

Proper Noun:

Proper noun is used to name a specific person, place, animal, things or idea.

Examples: -

London

Ferrari

More Examples: -

Harry Potter, Robin Hood, Paris, Japan, America, Mother's Day, December, Sunday, Niagara Fall, Lake Michigan, Mount Fuji, Albert Einstein

Concrete noun:

Concrete noun describes something that you can experience through your five physical senses.

You can *see, hear, touch, taste or smell.*

Examples: -

Flower

Books

More Examples: - Car, Cake, Watch, Dress, Shoes, Sheep, Cows, Umbrella,

Abstract noun:

Abstract noun describes something that you **cannot** see, hear, touch, taste or smell.

Examples: -

Happiness

Peace

More Examples: -Hate, Trust, Honesty, Faith, Wisdom, Joy, Anger

Countable noun: -

Countable noun is a word which can be counted.

Example: -

An apple

A dog

More Examples: -Bag, Truck, Bus, Restaurant, Airplane, Pen, Pencil, Children, Nails, Fish

Uncountable noun: - An uncountable noun can't be counted.

Example: -

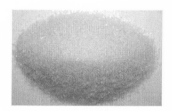

Sugar

More Examples: - Cereal, Bread, Salt, Soup, Juice, Rice, Jam, Milk, Cheese, Water

Collective noun: -

Collective nouns are words for groups of people, animals or things.

Example: -

A bunch of Keys

A collection of Books

More Examples: - A deck of cards, A pod of whales, A pride of lions, A herd of cattle, A set of stamps, A team of Players, A class of Pupils

Singular noun: -

A singular noun names one person, place, thing or idea.
Example: -

A Boy

A cat

More Examples: - A clock, A bell, A rat, A computer, An envelope, An orange, A bus

Plural Noun: -

A plural noun names more than one person, place, thing, place or idea.
Example: -

Potatoes

Balloons

More Examples: - Hats, Fishes, Feet, Bats, People, Mittens, Books, Coins, Toys, bicycles,

Most singular nouns form the plural by adding -s.
Examples:

Singular	Plural
Book	Books
Cat	Cats
Toy	Toys
Bat	Bats

A singular noun ending in s, x, z, ch, sh makes the plural by adding-es.

Singular	Plural
Box	Boxes
Wish	Wishes
Fish	Fishes
Watch	Watches

A singular noun ending in a consonant and then y makes the plural by dropping the y and adding-ies. If there is a vowel before the y, you just add 's'.

Singular	Plural
Baby	Babies
City	Cities
Party	Parties
Day	Days
Tray	Trays

Noun Exercise

Mark the correct category of the given noun.

1. Army

a) Common   b) Collective

c)Material   d) Abstract

2. Happiness

a) Common   b) Collective

c) Material   d) Abstract

3. Baby

a) Common   b) Collective

c)Material   d) Abstract

4. Magazine

a) Common   b) Collective

c) Material   d) Abstract

Circle the noun if it is a *concrete noun* and underline the noun if it is an *abstract noun*.

   1.Bob was given an award for his courage.
   2.This table is broken.
   3.Merry thinks that happiness is the most important thing in life.

4.Peter dropped his phone with a crash.
5.Time is a great teacher.
6.Harry's art teacher applauded his creativity.
7.Mia accidentally stubbed her toe on the table.

Underline the common noun in these sentences.

The phone is ringing.
My mother is a teacher.
I don't like eating apples.
Here is a gift for you.
My brother likes eating vegetables.
The little bird is sitting on a tree.

Here is a mixed bag of words. Put each word under its correct heading.

Doctor	crocodile	bus	camel
car	sea	France	plumber
parrot	letters	pigeon	tiger
mother	school	flower	Ice-cream

People	Place	Animal	Thing
-------------	------------	------------	------------
-------------	-----------	------------	--------------
-------------	--------------	-------------	--------------
--------------	-------------	--------------	--------------

Underline the Proper noun in these sentences.

1.My grandfather is a professor.
2.Miss Julie is reading a book.
3.We are going to Europe in July.
4.This Monday is holiday.

5.My friends are going to Point Pleasant beach.

6.In summer vacation, we are going to Disneyland.

Here is a mixed bag of words. Put each word under its correct heading.

Dr Chang	Women	Hotel	Marina Beach	Month	February
Hotel Grand	Bank	Miss Polly	Bank of America	Doll	Rice

Common Noun   **Proper noun**

--------------   ----------------

--------------   ----------------

--------------   ----------------

--------------   ------------------

--------------   ------------------

Make these words into plurals. Remember the RULE!

1. toy = toys

2. library = _____

3. holiday = _____

4. family = _____

5. diary = _____

6. trolley = _____

7. jockey = _____

8. allergy = _____

9. factory = _____

10. party = _____

Chapter-2

PRONOUN

Definition: -
Pronoun is a word that substitutes a noun. Generally, they refer to another word or words in the sentence.

Pronoun Examples:-

He, she, his, they, we, us, me, my, mine, I, you, it, ours, your, your, hers, her, its, their, theirs

Types of pronouns:

Personal pronoun
Demonstrative pronoun
Interrogative pronoun
Indefinite pronoun
Possessive pronoun
Reciprocal pronoun
Relative pronoun
Reflexive pronoun
Intensive pronoun

Personal Pronoun:
The word *I, We, You, He, She, They, it* are called personal pronouns. They take the place of nouns and used as the subject of verb in a sentence.

There are two cases of personal pronouns: **subject pronouns and object pronouns.**

Subject pronouns include *I, you, she, he, it, we, they*. Subject pronouns replace the name of the subject in the sentence. For example:

Examples: -

My name is Jack. **I** am a student.

This is my friend **John**. **He** is a smart boy.
This is my **mother**. **She** is a teacher.
Good morning **students**. **You** may sit down now.
Peter and Paul are my friend. **We** play together.

Object pronouns include ***me, you, her, him, it, us, them***. Object pronouns take the place of the object in the sentence (that is, the noun that receives the action in a sentence). Object pronouns are used as both direct objects and indirect objects.

Examples:

Merry is nice to all. Everybody likes **her.**

I am teaching a new chapter. Please look at **me**.

Jenny, I told you to wash **your** hand.

Tom and I are swimming, the lifeguard is watching **us.**

Mike and Mia, Dad is waiting for **you** !

Pick your **books** and put **them** on study table.

Demonstrative Pronoun:
The word ***this, these, that and those*** are called demonstrative pronouns.

This and these are used when you point things near you. That and those are used when you point things farther away.

Singular	Plural
This	These
That	Those

Examples: -

That is your book.

This is my dog
This is my nose.
That is your bag.
Please give me one of **those.**
These are nice shoes.

Interrogative pronoun:

The **words who, whom, whose, what, which** are called interrogative pronouns.
These pronouns are used to ask questions.

Examples: -
Whom are you playing with?
Which of these books is yours?
Whose is this bag?
What is the time now?
Who are you?
Note:
Who can be used as object of a verb as well as the subject.

Whom is used only as the object.

Indefinite pronoun:

Indefinite pronouns are those referring to unspecified objects, beings, or places. They are called indefinite because they do not indicate the exact object, being, or place to which they refer.

Indefinite pronouns include *any, anybody, anyone, either, neither, nobody, no, someone, some; every, all, each, several, enough, many, and much*.

I would like to go **somewhere** this summer.

Someone gave me this book.

There is **nothing** to do.

He looked **everywhere** for his car key.

Everybody enjoyed the concert.

If Michael can't come, we'll ask somebody **else**.

You can choose **anything** from the menu.

The doorbell rang but there was **no one** at home.

Possessive pronoun:

A possessive pronoun is used to avoid repeating information that has already been made clear. These useful pronouns make sentences less confusing and clear.

Yours, mine, theirs, ours, hers, his, its are used as Possessive pronouns.

Number	Person	Possessive Pronoun
Singular	1st(I)	Mine
	2nd(You)	Yours
	3rd(He/She/It)	His / Her/ Its
Plural	1st(We)	Ours
	2nd(You)	Yours
	3rd(They)	Theirs

Examples:

This cat is mine, not yours.

The house on the corner is theirs.

Lots of our friends were at the party.

The ring is hers.
This dessert is mine, but you can have it.
Your car is a lot faster than mine.
Reciprocal pronoun:
A reciprocal pronoun is a pronoun used to identify an action or feeling that is reciprocated. Any time something is done or given in return, reciprocal pronouns are used. There are only two reciprocal pronouns in the English language: each other and one another. Each other is used when referencing two nouns, and one another refers to three or more nouns.

Examples:

Both teams played hard against *each other*.

The boats were bumping against *each other* in the storm.

The students congratulated *one another*.

Why do you question *each other*?

Tom and Terry were talking to *each other* in the class.

The students helped *one another* to perform the group experiment.

Relative pronoun:

A relative pronoun marks a relative clause; it has the same referent in the main clause of a sentence that the relative modifies.
In English the following are the most common relative pronouns: *which, that, whose, whoever, whomever, who and whom.*

Examples:

This is the book *that* everyone is talking about.

I have a friend *whose* cat is annoying.

This is Bob, *whom* you met at our house last year.

We had pizza for our dinner, **which** is my favorite food.

That's the dog **who** doesn't like me.

Reflexive Pronoun:

A reflexive pronoun is used when the object of a sentence is the same as the subject. Each personal pronoun (such as I, you, he, she, it) has its own reflexive form.

The word **myself, himself, herself, itself, yourself, themselves, ourselves, yourselves** are reflexive pronouns. We use reflexive pronoun when we want to refer the subject of the sentence.

Subject	Reflexive Pronoun
I	myself
You	yourself
He	himself
She	herself
It	itself
You	yourself
Our	ourselves
You(plural)	yourselves
Them	themselves

Examples: -

I am teaching **myself** to play the piano.

Ben built a boat for **himself.**

The dog scratched itself.

Babies are too young to look after **themselves.**

Jill read to **herself.**

Come on **friends,** find a seat for **yourselves.**

My father and I painted the house **by ourselves.**

She was feeling very sorry for **herself**.

Intensive pronoun:
An intensive pronoun is almost identical to a reflexive pronoun. It is defined as a pronoun that ends in self or selves and places emphasis on its antecedent by referring back to another noun or pronoun used earlier in the sentence.

An intensive pronoun adds emphasis to a statement . Myself, yourself, himself, herself, ourselves, yourselves, themselves are used both as reflexive pronouns as well as intensive pronouns. But an intensive pronoun is different from a reflexive pronoun, as intensive pronoun can be removed without altering the meaning of the sentence.

Examples:

We ourselves baked the cake.

She will do it *herself.*

You yourselves can win this game.

The dog opened the cupboard *itself*.

The boys cooked the meal *themselves.*

EXERCISES

Select the pronoun which can best replace the underlined noun:

1. My sister isn't well. Dad is taking <u>my sister</u> to see a doctor.

a) She   b) her   c) They.........c) It

2. All of us have completed our work. <u>All of us </u>can play now.

a) she   b) We   c) They   c) It

3. John and Jack are playing football. <u>John and Jack </u>enjoy this game very much.

a) He   b) We   c) They   c) Them

4." Do you know Mr. Alex "? "Yes, I know <u>Mr. Alex</u> very well".

a) He   b) his   c) Him   c) Them

Choose the best answer to complete each sentence.

1. This is _____ speaking.

a) He   b) John   c) Him   c) He John

2. May _____ borrow your pen?

a) I   b) You   c) me   c) mine

3. The dog chewed on ------------------ favorite toy.

a) its   b) it's   c) its'   c) his

4. I am not convinced, I know --------------------------- are mere excuses.

a) This   b) These   c) That   c) Those

5. Stop boasting about ------------------- all the time.

a) Himself   b) herself   c) themselves   c) yourself

6. I am annoyed with ---------------------------- for the mistakes I have committed.

a) Himself   b) herself   c) themselves   c) myself

Write the correct interrogative pronouns in the blanks to complete the sentences:

1 _____ is this car in front of our house?

2 _____ invented the motor engine?

3 _____ old, are you?

4 _____ do you wish to speak to?

5 _____ of them do you think will win the race?

Fill in the blanks with the correct pronouns.

1. John and Jack are brothers. _____ share a bedroom together.

2. Mia isn't well. Dad is taking _____ to see a doctor.

3. My uncle is a teacher. _____ teaches English.

4. All his students like _____ very much.

5. Children, _____ are making too much noise!

6. Who are those people? Where are _____ from?

7. Mom is a doctor. _____ works in a hospital.

8. The sky is getting dark. _____ is going to rain.

9. John, we are all waiting for _____. Are you coming with _____?

10. May _____ borrow your pen?

11. Yes, of course. When can you return _____ to _____?

12. What are _____ reading, Jenny?

Write the correct interrogative pronouns in the blanks to complete the sentences:

1. _____ is the matter with you?

2. _____ invented the computer?

3. _____ of the bags is heavier?

4. _____ do you wish to speak to?

5. _____ is this car in front of our house?

6. _____ knows the answer?

7. _____ came first, the chicken or the egg?

8 ._____ would you like to drink?

9. _____ of them do you think look better?

10. _____ is the word for a stamp collector?

Complete the following sentences using the correct form of the pronoun given in the brackets.

1. Why are you shouting at _____ ? (I)

2. We are waiting for _____. (they)

3. He shouldn't have done this to _____. (you)

4. He loves _____ parents more than anyone else. (he)

5. We didn't expect this from _____ . (he)

6. _____ parents live abroad. (I)

7. He wants to marry _____ .(she)

8. The dog is happy. It has had _____breakfast. (it)

9. We are moving to _____ new home next month. (we)

10. He has never been to the country where _____ parents were born. (he)

11. Between you and _____I don't trust him. (I)

12. We are waiting for _____ . (she)

Choose the correct Interrogative pronouns

1. _____one of you is coming to my house later?

(a) Who (b) Which (c) Why (d) How

2. _____ are you going to get home from work?

(a) Which (b) Who (c) How (d) What

3. _____ is that guy talking to your sister?

(a) Which (b) Whose (c) Who (d) Whom

4. She wants to know _____ you like your coffee.

(a) how (b) what (c) which (d) who

5. Let me know _____ you hear from your mother.

(a) who (b) which (c) whose (d) when

6. _____would you like on your hamburger?

(a) How (b) What (c) When (d) Which

7. _____ dog is that?

(a) Who (b) When (c) Whose (d) Where

8. This is _____ I want to be when I grow up.

(a) why (b) when (c) which (d) what

9. My mother is the one_____ sings on TV every morning.

(a) whom (b) which (c) who (d) whose

10. _____shoes are those?

(a) Why (b) Whose (c) Whom (d) Who

Choose the correct Possessive pronouns

1. Mia left .... notebook on the bus.

(a) her (b) yours (c) his

2. The colorful picture of the flowers is ....

(a) their (b) your (c) mine

3. The proud parents brought home .... new baby girl.

(a) his (b) her (c) their

4. Jack strummed .... guitar and invited everyone to sing.

(a) his (b) its (c) her

5. The computer quickly stores information on .... huge memory.

(a) yours (b) theirs (c) its

6.These warm chocolate chip cookies melt in .... mouth.

(a) its (b) your (c) yours

7. Is .... seat belt always fastened?

(a) your (b) mine (c) its

8. The fluffy brown puppy is ....

(a) its (b) my (c) theirs

9 .... hand shot up when the teacher asked for volunteers.

 (a) Their (b) Her (c) Mine

10. I didn't get a cheeseburger, so I tasted ....

 (a) mine (b) its (c) hers

Chapter-3

VERB

Definition: -

A verb is a word that expresses an action or a state of being.
Verbs are a necessary component of all sentences.

Types of verb:

Action verb & Stative verb
Main verb & Auxiliary verb/helping verb
Regular & Irregular verb
Transitive & Intransitive verb

Action verb

An action verb is a verb that the subject can do.

Example:

Dance

Walk

More Examples: - Cook, Eat, Break, Work, Ride, Drive, Bring, Fetch, Jump, Swim

Stative verb

Stative verbs are verbs that express a state rather than an action. They usually relate to thoughts, emotions, relationships, senses, states of being and measurements.

More Examples: - Hate, Hope, Hear, Want, Need, Agree, Believe, Belong, Realize, Promise, See, Miss, Love, Smell

Main verb

Main verbs are those verbs that can stand on their own in sentences. They do not need the help of another verb to make a sentence meaningful. A main verb directly tells you what the subject of a sentence does.

Examples:

Merry **bakes** cookies.
Mia **fed** the cat.
Jenny **feels** confused.
George **mails** a letter.
The boy **eats** five meals a day.
Tom helped Sam.

Auxiliary verbs

These are verbs that are used with other verbs to make meaningful sentences. They are also called helping verbs.

The most common auxiliary verbs are *am, is, are, was, were, be, being, been, have, has, had, do, does, did, could, should, would, can, shall, will, may, might, must*

Examples:

Jim **is** writing a book.
I am having a cup of coffee.

He **has** done the work.
We **will** be there in a minute.

Tom **has** bought a new shirt.
I **have** purchased a new pair of shoes.
 I **don't** study at night.
 My mother **is** baking chocolate muffins today.
 I **did** not eat the leftover pizza.
 Did you visit Chicago last Sunday?
 Do you like the movie?
 Would you help me to find my book?
 Are you coming to my party?
 Does Sam write all his own reports?

Regular verb

A regular verb is a verb that forms its past tense and past participle by adding -ed to the base form. Most English verbs are regular.

Example: -

 We **visited** New York last week.
 Mom **cooked** pasta for dinner.
 Merry **baked** cookies for us.
 Harry **pushed** Mike.
 They **walked** to school together.
 I **reached** there by train.
 Who **closed** all the windows?
 We **waited** long to visit that place.

Irregular verb

Irregular verbs are verbs which do not follow normal rules for conjugation.

There is no formula to predict how an irregular verb will form its past-tense and past-participle forms. There are over 250 irregular verbs in English. Although they do not follow a formula, there are some common irregular forms. Some of these forms are:

break, broke, broken
cut, cut, cut
run, ran, run
meet, met, met
come, came, come
repay, repaid, repaid
swim, swam, swum
be was/ were been

Examples:

Max **got** a bike on his birthday.

I **lost** my favorite book.

I **heard** a loud noise.

We **sold** our car last week.

My mother met her old friend in a shopping center.

Hennery **ate** sweets.

Transitive verb

A transitive verb is one that is used with an object: a noun, phrase, or pronoun that refers to the person or thing that is affected by the action of the verb.

Examples:

My father left his car key on the table.

The boy **wants** cookies.

Merry **loves** pets.

Mathew thanked Mike.

Please **buy** me a dog !

He **cleaned** his car.

I **admire** your courage.

She **carried** the bags.

Intransitive verb

An intransitive verb does not have an object.

Examples:

We laughed uncontrollably.

The baby was crying.

My father works for a large firm in New York.

We talked for hours.

Every single student read this book.

The crowd demonstrated outside the theatre.

Exercises

Underline the verb

1. The dogs buried their bones.

2. Heather's cat chased a very, large bird.

3. Mark and his father hunted for treasures.

4. John bought tickets for the game.

5. Linda and her brother built a treehouse.

6. The people clapped loudly at the play.

7. Robert saved money for a new bicycle.

8. Susan rode her horse every day.

9. Terri paid for the movie.

10. Mike shoveled the snow.

11. Andy baked a birthday cake.

12. Paul changed the light bulb.

Circle the action verb. and underline the stative Verb

Mind	Agree	Seem	Appear
Eat	Know	Hear	Own
Doubt	Imagine	Shout	Swim
Cry	Drink	Pull	Remember

In each sentence, circle the main verb and underline the Auxiliary verbs.

1.Mr. Alex was talking about his new car.

2.The girl had asked for ice cream.

3.Children are enjoying the cupcakes.

4.We are taking pizza for friends.

5.My grandmother will need some help.

6. Everyone has enjoyed the party.

In below sentences, circle the transitive verb and underline the intransitive verb.

1.She loves animals.

2.We talked for hours.

3.I couldn't face him today.

4.I admire your courage.

5.We need to maintain product quality.

6.The baby was crying.

7.They laughed uncontrollably.

8.I work for a large firm in Paris.

In each sentence, underline the auxiliary verbs.

I am hungry.

They will help you.

We do not know his address.

My friend Amy does a lot of sports.

How much is it?

I am reading an interesting book at the moment.

Will you be there?

She has never been to London.

Does he speak English?

They have a cat and a dog.

Chapter-4

ADVERB

Definition: -

A word that describes or gives more information about a verb, adjective or phrase.

An adverb answers the question *when? where? how? how much? how long? or how often?*

Examples:

> We are going to visit New York **soon.**
> The young man played music **loudly.**
> I will call you **later**.
> The man walked **slowly** down the road.
> We go to park **regularly**.

Types of Adverbs

Adverb of Time

Adverb of Manner

Adverb of Place

Adverb of Degree

Adverb of Frequency

Adverb of Time

An adverb of time provides more information about when a verb takes place. Adverb of time tells you the time of occurrence of an incident and also its duration and frequency.

Adverbs of time show us **when, how long and how often** an action occurs.

List of commonly used adverbs of time:

When: *afterwards, soon, today, yesterday, later, now, last year, Saturday, Sunday, next week*

How long: *since, all hours, all day, not long, for a while, since last year, for three days, for a week, for several years, for two centuries*

How often: *regularly, usually, sometimes, frequently, occasionally, never, often, yearly*

Examples: -

My brother goes to Gym E**very day**.

My father **recently** bought a new car.

My school will reopen on **Monday.**

Today is a very hot day.

Are you coming to school **tomorrow**?

Jim is **still** waiting to see the dentist.

Adverb of Place

Adverbs of place illustrate where the verb is happening. It's usually placed after the main verb or object, or at the end of the sentence.

List of commonly used adverbs of place:

Here	There	In	Out
Inside	Outside	Above	Below

No where	Everywhere	Into	Away
Downstairs	Upstairs	Underground	Next door

Examples:

Children are playing **downstairs.**

Today I lost my pen somewhere.

We went into the cave, and there were bats **everywhere**!

There aren't any Pokémon **here,** let's look somewhere else.

The miners are working **underground.**

It's raining, let's go **inside**.

The plane moves **upwards** on full thrust.

Adverbs of Manner

Adverbs of manner are used to tell us the way or how something is done.

Adverbs of manner are probably the most common of all adverbs. They're easy to spot too. Most of them will end in **–ly.**

List of commonly used adverbs of manner:

angrily , anxiously, badly, beautifully, calmly, carefully, carelessly, cautiously, cheerfully, clearly, closely, correctly, deliberately, eagerly, easily, enthusiastically, fondly, frankly, naturally, neatly, noisily, obediently, patiently, perfectly, politely

Examples: -

They played music **loudly.**

He plays the flute **beautifully.**

You have all answered **correctly**

The driver braked **suddenly**.

Today I rested **lazily** on the sofa.

Should we dress **casually**?

Adverbs of Degree

Adverbs of degree explain the level or intensity of a verb, adjective, or even another adverb.

List of commonly used adverbs of degree:

Almost , Absolutely , Awfully , Badly, Barely , completely, decidedly, deeply, enough , enormously , entirely, extremely, fairly, far, fully, greatly, incredibly, indeed, intensely, just, least, less, little, lots, most, much, nearly , perfectly, positively, practically , pretty, purely, quite, rather, really, scarcely , simply , somewhat, strongly, terribly, thoroughly, too, totally , utterly, very, virtually

Examples: -

The soup is **very** hot.

The shoes are **too** big for my sister.

My family is **so** excited for Christmas celebration!
I was **simply** furious when I heard the noise
Aren't you hungry? You've **hardly** touched your dinner.
I'm **so** excited to see the new James Bond movie!
Today it's **extremely** cold outside.

Adverbs of Frequency

Adverbs of frequency explain how often the verb occurs. They're often placed directly before the main verb of a sentence.

List of commonly used adverbs of frequency:

always , usually, often, normally, occasionally, sometimes, seldom ,never, hardly, ever,   constantly, continually, frequently, infrequently, intermittently, periodically, rarely, regularly, generally, now and then, almost never, eventually, quarterly, weekly, later, then

Example: -
I **rarely** eat fast food these days.
I **hardly** watch TV.
Tom **usually** takes his dog for a walk before breakfast.
They **always** go to the same restaurant every Friday.
I **hardly** play video games.
We should **never** tell a lie.
Sometimes I do exercise.

Exercises

Select the adverb in the following sentences

1. You are quite wrong in this matter.

A. You   B. Quite

C. Wrong   D. Matter

2. The child cried loudly.

A. The   B. Cried

C. loudly   D. child

3. Mr. Jose formerly lived in California.

A. Formerly   B. Lived

C. California   D. In

Fill in the blanks with the most suitable adverb:

1. Our art teacher was ----------------- lost in thought.

 a) generally   b) quickly   c) very   d) heavily

2. We are ---------- tired after the trekking.

a) more   b) too   c) very   d) much

3. Have you seen our cat --------?

a) somewhere   b) anywhere   c) everywhere   d) nowhere

4. They discussed the matter ------------.

a) hardly   b) briefly   c) cleanly   d) angrily

5. Merry and I ------------ meet each other these days.

a) rather   b) rarely   c) very   d) more

Underline the Adverb in the below sentences.

1.The train tried to plow through the snow earlier.

2.Snow fell everywhere.

3.People were trapped inside.

4.The water inside has frozen.

5.Andew Greeted us warmly.

6.Mike and Mia dove rapidly under a big wave.

7.They swam very slowly.

8.A dolphin nudged Jack very gently.

Chapter- 5

ADJECTIVE

Definition: -

An adjective is a word that describes or clarifies a noun. Adjectives describe nouns by giving some information about an object's size, shape, age, color, origin or material.

Examples: -

It's a *big* table. (size)

It's a *round* table. (shape)

It's an *old* table. (age)

It's a *brown* table. (color)

It's a *wooden* table. (material)

It's a *lovely* table. (opinion)

It's a *broken* table. (observation)

It's a *coffee* table. (purpose)

Types of adjectives-

> *Qualitative/ Descriptive*
> *Quantitative*
> *Possessive*
> *Demonstrative*
> *Distributive*
> *Interrogative*

Qualitative/ Descriptive

The descriptive adjectives can be simply defined as the type of adjectives that are used to express the condition, shape, size, value and color of a noun. They are used to provide more information to a noun by describing or modifying it.

It describes the

Condition like hot, cold, rainy, sunny

Shapes like round, rectangular, square, oval

Size like small, big, thin, long

Value like beautiful, smart, shy, rich, poor

Color like red, blue, brown, yellow, white

Examples: -

We ate some **delicious** food.

She has a **beautiful** voice.

You should always eat **green** leafy vegetables.
Give me that **big** slice of pizza.
Alex is a **nice** boy.
My father is a **hard-working** person.
We caught a running kangaroo.
Don't eat in that **broken** plate.

Quantitative Adjective

Quantitative Adjectives are those Adjectives which describe the measurement. As the name suggests, this kind of adjective answers the question, "How many?" or "How much?"

List of commonly used quantitative adjectives are:

Some, few, little, most, all, no, enough, any, whole, sufficient, none

Examples:

I ate **some** rice.
He ate **half** of my burger.

I do not have **any** chocolates in my bag.

Four students were expelled from the school.

Jack has **many** books in his backpack.

John completed the **whole** task.

I have **sufficient** money for shopping.

There was **no** milk in the jar.

Possessive Adjective

This kind of adjectives shows ownership or possession. Aside from that, possessive adjectives always come before the noun.

List of commonly used possessive adjectives are:

My, your, his, her, its, our, their, whose

Examples:

The tiger is chasing **its** prey.
My mother is a doctor.
Bob sold **his** dog.
That's **our** house.
I lent **my** guitar to my friend.
Paul, **your** handwriting is difficult to read.

The doctor asked **his** patient to open **her** mouth.

What is the Difference Between Possessive Adjectives and Possessive Pronouns?

Although the possessive adjectives and possessive pronouns are closely related and can sometimes be confusing, it is actually very easy to differentiate one from the other. You have to remember that possessive pronouns are used to replace the noun and possessive adjectives are used to describe the noun.

Use possessive adjectives with nouns or noun phrases. Use possessive pronouns alone. Don't use them with nouns or noun phrases.

Examples :

Possessive adjectives	Possessive nouns
1. **My** computer is on the table.	1.The computer on the table is **mine.**
2. It is **her** book.	2. The book is **hers**.
3. **Our** house is beautiful.	3. The beautiful house is **ours.**

Demonstrative Adjectives

Demonstrative adjectives point out pronouns and nouns, and always come before the words they are referring to.

List of commonly used demonstrative adjectives are:

This, That, These, those

Examples:

This ice cream is delicious.
I did not enjoy **that** book.

I used to buy **this** kind of shirts.
What is **that** animal?
Bring me **those** books.
Do you like **these** toys?

Distributive adjectives

Adjectives which are used to refer people or things individually among many are called distributive adjectives.

List of commonly used distributive adjectives are:

Each, every, either, neither, any, one

Examples: -

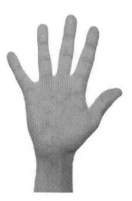

Each hand has five fingers.

My grand father used to call me **every** day.

Either of these movies would be interesting to me.

Neither of the two men is trustworthy.

Is there **any** coffee in the pot?

Any one of you can participate in the competition.

Interrogative Adjective

Interrogative adjectives modify nouns and are used in interrogative sentences.

List of commonly used interrogative adjectives are:

What, Whose, Where, Why, How, Which

Examples:

What time is it?

Whose footprints are these?

What a beautiful flower is this.

Which road leads to the park?

Whose bag is this?

What book are you reading?

Why did he absent today?

Exercises

Fill in the blanks with suitable adjectives.

Playful	kind	poor	free
sweet	empty	hot	healthy

1. Many _____ people have no home.

2.It is very ------ in summer.

3.The company is giving ------ offer to the customers.

4.The chocolate is very……….

5.The children are very ……….

6.We should exercise to keep ……….

7.You are so …….

8.There was an ------ room upstairs.

Select the adjectives in the following sentences.

1. The girl is wearing a beautiful gown.

a) Gown   b) wearing c) beautiful d) girl

2. What is that bird?

a) What   b) is   c) bird   d) that

3. Each student was asked to complete the task.

a) Each   b) asked   c) to   d) task

4. I have a little knowledge about computing.

a) have   b) about   c) little   d) computing

5. Harry ate all the ice cream happily.

a) Ate   b) all   c) ice cream   d) happily

Chapter- 6

ARTICLES

Definition: -

An article is a word that gives some information about a noun. It defines a noun as specific or unspecific.

Types of articles-

Indefinite (a, an)
Definite (the)

Indefinite article:

The words **a and an** are called indefinite articles. You can use them with singular nouns to talk about any single person or thing. The article **an** is usually used before words beginning with vowels (a, e, i, o, u). The article **a** is used before words beginning with consonants.

Examples: -

Please give me **a** glass of water.

He is **a** teacher

My friend bought **a** new house.

I am reading **a** book.

This is **a** picture of **an** elephant

We are looking for **an** apartment.

It was such **a** fine day!

Mary needs **a** passport.

He is **an** actor while his wife is **a** doctor.

A dog is a friendly animal.

Please give me **an** ice cube.

Mom bought me **a** new dress today.

You will need **an** umbrella when you go out.

She eats **an** apple **a** day.

Definite article:

The definite article is used to refer to a particular member of a group or class. It may be something that the speaker has already mentioned, or it may be something uniquely specified. There is one definite article in English, for both singular and plural nouns, that is *"The"*.

Examples:

Have you read **the** newspaper?

The telephone is ringing.

The road is very busy today.

Turn on **the** radio!

The general was invited to **the** party.

 I went to see **the** doctor.

The professor was never late.

Have you locked **the** door?

Are you going to **the** party this weekend?

My grandfather is sitting in **the** garden.

Exercises

Fill in the blanks with a, an or the.

1.------- computer   2. --------- tree   3.------ sun   4. ------- orange

5. ------- moon   6. ----- ice cream   7. ------ apple   8.----- jacket

9.------ umbrellas   10.----- tiger   11. ----- elephant   12.---- tomato

13.---- dog   14.---- apron   15. ---- banana   16.--- page

Fill in the blanks with a, an or the.

1.John wanted to read a / an /the comic book.

2. He studies in   a/an/the university.

3.Please give me a/an/the book of your choice.

4.A/an/the earth is round.

5. I quickly ate the / an /a cookies.

6. A /an/the sun rises in the east.

7. Danny put a / an /the orange on his yogurt.

8. A / an/ the year ago I visited Paris.

9. A/ an/ the January is the first month of a year.

10. He likes to read a/ an / the short stories.

Write a, an or the in the blanks to complete the sentences.

1. There is _____ rainbow in _____ sky.

2. Who is _____ boy outside _____ house?

3. _____ teacher gave John_____ book.

4. Jack opened _____ door to let _____ guest in.

5. Peter is _____ tallest boy in _____ class.

6. What's _____ largest animal in _____ world?

7. There's _____ nest in _____ tree.

8. _____ earth is bigger than _____ mars.

Chapter- 7

PREPOSITION

Definition: -

A preposition is a word used to link nouns, pronouns, or phrases to other words within a sentence. Prepositions are usually short words, and they are normally placed directly in front of nouns.

List of Common Prepositions

above	about	across	along	among,	around	at
against	before	behind	below	beneath	beside	between
beyond	by	down	during	except	for	from
in	inside	into	like	near	of	off
on	since	to	toward	through	under	until
up	upon	with	within			

Types of preposition: -

Preposition of place

Preposition of time

Preposition of direction or movement

Prepositions of Agent

Prepositions of Instruments, devices or Machines

Preposition of place
A preposition of place is a preposition which is used to refer to a place where something or someone is located.

Most common preposition of place are
At, In, On

At tells us that the following noun is located at a specific point or location. It shows an exact position.

In tells us the noun is in an enclosed space (surround or closed off on all sides). Basically, when something is inside something.

On tells us that the following noun is located on a surface. Use on when one thing is attached to or touching something.
Examples: -

Please place the bouquet on the table.

I'm growing tomatoes **in** my garden.

There is a fly **on** the table.

I was born **in** England.

Jessie waited for Jim **at** the corner.

The mall is located **at** the intersection of Main Street and Third Avenue.

We spent a quiet evening **at** home.

Marie was born **in** France.

I was so tired that I took a nap **in** the car.

I really wish you would stop throwing your dirty clothes **on** the floor.

Preposition of time

A preposition of time is a preposition that allows you to discuss a specific time such as a date on the calendar, one of the days of the week, or the actual time something takes place. Prepositions of time are the same words as prepositions of place, however they are used in a different way. You can easily distinguish these prepositions, as they always discuss times rather than places.

At – This preposition of time is used to discuss clock times, holidays and festivals, and other very specific time frames including exceptions, such as "at night."

In – This preposition of time is used to discuss months, seasons, years, centuries, general times of day, and longer periods of time such as "in the past."

On – This preposition of time is used to discuss certain days of the week or portions of days of the week, specific dates, and special days such as "on New Year's Day."

Examples :

We always have a huge celebration on my birthday.

We're going bowling *on* Friday night.

My birthday falls **in** January.

Birds often migrate *in* spring and autumn.

My great-grandmother was born **in** 1906.

Breakfast is a meal which is generally eaten **in** the morning.

My parents grew up **in** the 1960s.

My vacation ends **on** Monday.

My brother John was born **on** September 3rd.

Meet me **at** 7:30.

The town is always well-decorated **at** Christmastime.

Now that my grandfather is older, he no longer drives **at** night.

Preposition of direction or movement

Preposition of direction & Movement tells where to go or where to put something. Prepositions of direction show us to where or in which direction something moves.

Most common preposition of direction or movement are:

Across, against, along, around, away from, down, from, into, onto, out of, over, though, to, toward(s), under, up

Examples:
My brother riding his bike **up** hills.

I walk **to** school.

They came **to** the wedding.

Sofia flew **to** Canada.

The boat will take you **across** the river.

You must walk **across** the street at the crosswalk.

He's walking **along** the path.

The street runs **along** the seafront.

You must drive around the city center **to** reach the cinema.

Let's go for a walk **to** the park.

Don't go **into** the Principal's room.

We went **into** the shop on the corner.

We climbed **up** the mountain this morning.

Who is that woman running **towards** us?

Walk **towards** the sea and turn left at the first street.

You must turn on your lights when passing **through** the tunnel.

Prepositions of Agent

Preposition for agent is used for a thing which is a cause of another thing in the sentence. These prepositions are applied to indicate that an action conducted on a noun is caused by another noun, when used in a sentence.

Most common preposition of agent are:

By, With

Examples:

This book is written **by** Shakespeare.

She graduated **with** honors.

I'm going to New York next week **with** my parents.

She is writing **with** her blue pen.

The tub is filled **with** water

He was hit **by** a ball.

My father must be home **by** now.

The party hall was decorated **by** Jenny.

Prepositions of Instruments, devices or Machines

A preposition of instrument or device is used when describing certain technologies, machines, or devices. Typically, by refers to methods of transportation, whereas with and on describe the use of machines and other devices.

Most common preposition of Instruments, devices or machines are:

By, with, and on.

Example:

She comes **by** bus daily.

I opened the locked door **with** an old key.

May I finish my homework **on** your computer?

I returned home **by** ferry.

He broke the lock **with** a stone.

Exercises

Fill in the blanks with appropriate preposition

1. There is a beautiful pencil --------- the box.

a) in   b) about c) on   d) below

2.My friends agree .... my proposal.

a) in   b) with c) on   d) from

3.The dentist asked the children to take care -------- their teeth.

a) in   b) about   c) of   d) from

4.Be honest ----- all.

a) from   b) to   c) for   d) on

5. My vacation ends ----- Monday.

a) from   b) to   c) for   d) on

6. Jack was born -------- England.

a) from   b) in   c) to   d) on

7.There is a picture -------- the wall.

a) from   b) to   c) for   d) on

8. The bus arrived ------ 8:30 am.

a) in   b) on c) at d) from

9. John is extremely busy ------- his work.

a) of b) with   c) for d) to

10.The baby is hiding ------ the chair.

a) behind   b) in c) of   d) from

Underline the Preposition in the below sentences.

1. He's walking along the path.

2. Jill is running after the dog.

3.People are waiting at the bus stop.

4. I go to school by bus.

5. We have dinner at 7:30 pm.

6.There are 30 days in a month.

7. I was born in Chicago.

8.Why are you still in bed?

9. Let's go for a walk around the park.

10. The books are lying on the table.

Choose the correct prepositions of time:

At	above	about	after	before	behind	by

down   during   for from   in   in front of   of   on
out of   over   to   with

1. There were _____ a thousand people at the concert.

2. You must be _____ 18 in order to see the film.

3. We are travelling _____ the road.

4. He is suffering _____ an unknown illness.

5. I listened to the game _____ the radio.

6. How are you getting _____ at school?

7. Don't be impatient _____ us. We are trying!

8. Could I speak _____ Tom please?

9. We didn't see the whole performance because we left _____ the last act.

10. There were some beautiful pictures _____ the walls.

11. The march started in the park. _____ there we moved to City Hall.

12. Pessimism is bad _____ your health

13. He asked his mother _____ money.

14. I bought many things _____ my stay in New York.

15. My country is famous _____ historical sights.

16. I'm not _____ a hurry. I can wait.

17. Have you ever been _____ the theatre recently?

18. We arrived _____ the airport _____ time for the plane.

Chapter- 8

CONJUNCTION

A conjunction is a part of speech that is used to connect words, phrases, clauses, or sentences. Conjunctions are invariable grammar particle, and they may or may not stand between items they conjoin. The main job of a conjunction is to link together different parts of a sentence to help you connect or emphasize ideas, and form more complex and interesting sentences.

Types of Conjunctions:

Coordinating

Subordinating

Correlative

Coordinating Conjunctions

Coordinating conjunctions connect two words or groups of words with similar values. They may connect two words, two phrases, two independent clauses or two dependent clauses.

For example, in each of the following sentences the coordinating conjunction "and" connects equal words or groups of words:

Connects two words: John and Reggie stayed up all night practicing their guitars.

Connects two phrases: The squirrel scurried up the tree trunk and onto a low branch.

Connects two clauses: Several managers sat with their backs to us, and I could almost hear them snickering at us lowly workers.

It's a good idea to use the mnemonic **"FANBOYS"** to memorize coordinating conjunctions so you'll never forget them.

Most common coordinating conjunctions are:

For, And, Nor, But, Or, Yet, So

Examples of Coordinating Conjunctions: -

I am a vegetarian, **so** I don't eat any meat.
You can use a spoon **or** a fork to eat the cake.
My dog enjoys being bathed **but** hates getting his nails trimmed.
Bill refuses to eat peas, **nor** will he touch carrots.
His two favorite sports are football **and** tennis.
Thomas will be late to work, **for** he has a dental appointment

Subordinating conjunctions

Subordinating conjunctions connect two groups of words by making one into a subordinating clause. The subordinating clause acts as one huge adverb, answering the questions "when" or "why" about the main clause, or imposing conditions or opposition on it.

Most common Subordinating conjunctions are:

for, as, since, therefore, hence, as a result, consequently, though, due to, provided that, because , unless, as a result of, so/so that, once, while, when, whenever, where, wherever, before, and after, till, until, after, only, only-if, since, so, although, as if, as long as, etc.

Examples:

Merry decided to take a walk **because** she was getting bored at home. (why)
I can go shopping **after** I finish my study. (when)
I'll give you a dime **only if** you give me a dollar. (condition)
Although he never figured out why, Hanna winked on her way out the door. (opposition)
Because it was raining, I took my umbrella.

My elder brother drove my father's car **whenever** he was away.

Correlative conjunctions

Correlative conjunctions are always used in pairs. They are like coordinating

conjunctions because they join sentence elements that are similar in importance.

Most common correlative conjunctions are:

Both and, either or, neither nor, not only but also , whether or, not but, as/as, such that, as many as, rather than

Examples of Correlative Conjunctions:

Both Jon **and** his friends enjoyed the dolphin show.

Neither Paul **nor** Jack made the varsity team this year.

Not only, Rodney made the varsity team, **but** he **also** became one of the strongest players.

She is **both** intelligent **and** beautiful.

Jerry is **neither** rich **nor** famous.

He is **not only** intelligent, **but also** very funny.

Would you **rather** go shopping **or** spend the day at the beach?

This food is **both** delicious **and** healthy.

I will **either** go for biking **or** stay home and watch TV

Exercises

Underline the conjunctions in the below sentences.

1. Wherever the cat goes, her kittens follow.

2.The children were happy when they saw Santa Claus.

3. I asked for some bread and butter.

4. Wait here until I came back.

5. Take all your belongings when you leave the plane.

6. Dressy listened to the music while she was doing her homework.

7.She loves flowers but can't tell their names.

8.My father came late from work because it was raining heavily.

9.Don't talk while eating.

10.My grandfather is very old still he goes for morning walk daily.

Fill in the blanks with appropriate conjunction.

1. My brother loves animals. He just brought a puppy ---------- a kitten home with him.

a) or   b) and   c) both   d) nor

2. I'd like to thank you -------- the lovely gift.

a) for   b) because   c) and   d) yet

3. I want to go with you --------- I have go to work today.

a) so   b) and   c) but   d) yet

4. I'm getting good grades ---------- I study every day.

a) for   b) and   c) because   d) so

5. I tried to hit the nail ------------- hit my thumb instead.
a) so   b) and   c) but   d) yet

6. You can have peach ice cream ------------ a brownie sundae.

a) or   b) and   c) both   d) nor

7. My dad always worked hard ----------- he could afford the things we wanted.

a) so   b) and   c) but   d) yet

Chapter-9

CONTRACTIONS

A contraction is a shortened form of a group of words. Contractions are used in both written and oral communication. When a contraction is written in English, the omitted letters are replaced by an apostrophe.

ORIGINAL	CONTRACTION
are not	aren't
Cannot	can't
could not	couldn't
did not	didn't
does not	doesn't
do not	don't
had not	hadn't
has not	hasn't
have not	haven't
he had, he would	he'd
he will, he shall	he'll
he is, he has	he's
I had, I would	I'd
I will, I shall	I'll
I am	I'm
I have	I've
is not	isn't

it is, it has	it's
let us	let's
must not	mustn't
shall not	shan't
she had, she would	she'd
she will, she shall	she'll
she is, she has	she's
should not	shouldn't
that is, that has	that's
there is, there has	there's
they had, they would	they'd
they will, they shall	they'll
they are	they're
they have	they've
we had, we would	we'd
we are	we're
we have	we've
were not	weren't
what will, what shall	what'll
what are	what're
what is, what has	what's
what have	what've
where is, where has	where's
who had, who would	who'd

who will, who shall	who'll
who are	who're
who is, who has	who's
who have	who've
will not	won't
would not	wouldn't
you had, you would	you'd
you will, you shall	you'll
you are	you're
you have	you've

Chapter- 10

INTERJECTION

An interjection is a word that express a sudden, strong feeling such as surprise, pain or pleasure.

Examples of interjections.

a-ha	ahem	alas	amen	aw
bah	big deal	bingo	boo	boo hoo
bravo	brilliant	brrr	bull	bye (bye-bye)
cheers	cool	duh	dear me	darn
ouch	duck	eh	enjoy	excellent

fantastic	finally	for heaven's sake	foul	freeze
goodbye	gosh	great	ha	hello
hi	hip, hip, hooray	hmm	ho ho ho	hooray (hurray)
huh	ick	man	my goodness	no problem
nope	OK	Oh-no	oops	please
welcome	well	wow	yippee	yummy

Please check this out:

Our other best-selling books for kids are-

Most Popular Animal Quiz book for Kids: 100 amazing animal facts

Quiz Book for Kids: Science, History, Geography, Biology , Computer & Information Technology

Solar System & Space Science- Quiz for Kids : What You Know About Solar System

Know about Sharks: 100 Amazing Fun Facts with Pictures

Know About Whales:100+ Amazing & Interesting Fun Facts with Pictures: " Never known Before "- Whales facts

Know About Dinosaurs : 100 Amazing & Interesting Fun Facts with Pictures

Know About Kangaroos: Amazing & Interesting Facts with Pictures
Know About Penguins: 100+ Amazing Penguin Facts with Pictures

Know About Dolphins :100 Amazing Dolphin Facts with Pictures

100 Amazing Quiz Q & A About Penguin: Never Known Before Penguin Facts

English Grammar Practice Book for elementary kids: 1000+ Practice Questions with Answers

A to Z of English Tense: Learn English Tense in 2 Days

Our other kids' books are:

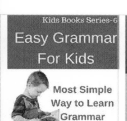

Kids Books Series-6
Easy Grammar For Kids
Most Simple Way to Learn Grammar
By Bandana Ojha

Kids Books series
Whales
100+ Amazing Fun Facts with Pictures

By Bandana

Kids Book Series - 4
Know About
Sharks
100 Amazing Fun Facts with Pictures
By Bandana Ojha

Kids Books Series
Dolphins
By Bandana

100 Amazing Fun Facts with Pictures

Kids Books Series-5
Penguins
Quiz Q & A Book with Pictures

By Bandana Ojha

Kids Books Series-9
Solar System & Space Science Quiz for Kids
By Bandana Ojha

Kids Books Series-7
Quiz For Kids
Science, History, Geography, Computer & Information Technology

200+ Q & A
A Must Read Book for Every Kid
By Bandana Ojha

Kids Books Series- 3
Penguins
100+ amazing Penguin Facts with Pictures
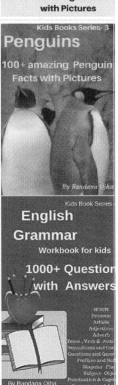
By Bandana Ojha

Kids Books Series
Animal Quiz for Kids
By Bandana

Kids Book Series-10
Know About
Kangaroos
By Bandana Ojha
Amazing & Interesting Facts with Pictures

Kids Book Series
Know About
Dinosaurs
Amazing Facts with Pics
By Bandana Ojha

Kids Book Series
English Grammar
Workbook for kids
1000+ Questions with Answers
By Bandana Ojha

NOUN
Pronoun
Article
Adjective
Adverb
Tense, Verb & Auxi
Prepositions and Con
Questions and Quer
Prefixes and Suff
Singular Plur
Subject-Obje
Punctuation & Capit
Synonyms and An

Made in the USA
Columbia, SC
18 March 2020